Growing Up in America-

A Primer for Youth-
Musings on making your dreams come true and more...

Ronald H. Bartalini

Sundie Enterprises
Since 1972

Copyright © 2016 by Ronald H. Bartalini
All rights reserved.

In accordance with the U.S. Copyright act of 1976, the scanning, uploading, and electronic sharing of any part of this book without the permission of the publisher is unlawful piracy and theft of the author's intellectual property. If you would like to use material from the book (other than for review purposes), prior written permission must be obtained from the publisher at permission:

Sundie Enterprises
P.O. Box 1274
Provo, Utah 84603-1274

ISBN 978-0-9859811-6-7
Library of Congress Control Number
2016903663
Bartalini, Ronald H.

Description: This book will show young people the steps necessary to make their dreams come true. In addition, you will learn how to be an effective leader and a trustworthy employee. Children and young people can also learn how to be examples for grown-ups to follow.

Dedication

*For my brother, Thomas Lee Roy,
and my sisters:
Patricia Ann and Anita Lynn, A.K.A.
Tommy, Patty and Binki, or T-Poy, Dorbi and
Binkerdilly*

Appreciation

My warmest thanks go to my friend and neighbor Bill Baker for his insightful and most helpful editing. Thank you Tate Feller for your expertise in solving a formatting problem.

Preface

If you are blessed to have a dream, hold on to it. Never give up, never let it go. Believe in your dream, believe in yourself, believe in God, and trust God to help you make your dream come true. God did not give you your dreams to let them collect dust in notebooks, or worse yet, to begin to rust in the back of your mind as something you will do some day. God gave you your dreams, to share with all of his children throughout the world. Now you must do the rest and get busy and make your dreams come true.

Here is the test to know if your dream comes from you or from God: Will your dream make the world a better place in which to live or will your dream only satisfy and help yourself?

Ten Suggestions for Getting the Most Out of This Book:

A.   Decide to Change Your Life

Did you know that making the decision to change your life for the better has the power to change your life for the better forever? If you decide now what you will not do, then when the time for making a decision comes, you will already know what you will do. You will not have to wait to think about what your decision will be. You will not have to hesitate to make a decision, you will have already made it.

B.   Visualize and Imagine-See the New You

Do you realize and understand that everyone who has ever amounted to anything once began just like you? First they were an infant, then a child, then a young adult, before they grew into adulthood. What separates some from the rest of the crowd? Perhaps it is just this simple, those who achieved greatness saw themselves as achieving distinction. They visualized and imagined themselves as already being the success they hoped for and that quality drove them to achieve the victory.

C. Do Not Compare Yourself to Other People

Most people will disappoint you. That is because we are not perfect. Compare yourself to the great Exemplar, even Jesus Christ. He is the only perfect person to walk the earth, and he will never disappoint you. He will always be there for you, to accept you as you are, and where you are spiritually, right now. He will always be reaching out and inviting you to come and follow him. Our beloved Savior's invitation is for all: "Come unto me, all ye that labor and are heavy laden and I will give you rest." (Matthew 11:28).

Follow the example of Christ in all of your comings and goings in this life. Ask yourself, "What would Jesus do?" When you respond similarly you will do well.

D. Read This Book with Your Family or with Friends

Oftentimes when we read in isolation we can miss some meanings and implications. Reading alone is a good thing and we should never stop doing that. However, I learned long ago, that everyone I will ever meet will know at least one thing that I do not know. They will also have had experiences I have not yet had.

E.   Invite Everyone in Your Group to Take a Turn Reading One or More Sub-headings As You Desire

It may be helpful for parents and children or friends of all ages to read this book together. This could be a way for youth to acquire some adult wisdom without having to wait until you are an adult. You cannot over-estimate the value of reading together and discussing the principles being taught as a group. When you read in a group setting, you may be able to share some experiences you have already had with someone much older.

F.   Discuss What Has Been Read

Even the youngest children can share their own thoughts, which can influence meaningfully.

G.   Go Out and Practice the Principle(s) Being Taught. Do It. Get It Done.

We learn more by doing than by listening. It is hoped, that reading this book will cause the hearer to take action. We learn from reading the Bible that "faith without works is dead." (James 2:20). That is a true principle. But knowledge without action is also dead and profits us nothing. We must get out and do small acts of kindness and not just talk or hear about it.

H.   Don't Be Afraid to Fail

You must go out into the world and not be afraid to embarrass yourself should you make a mistake or two, as you endeavor to make your dreams come true.

I.   Discuss Your Victories and Successes the Next Time You Meet As a Group

I am a big fan of feedback and opinions from friends and even strangers about my creative work. Their suggestions always seem to make my work better and I am grateful for them.

J.   Repeat the Process

You may have to go back and re-visit a certain principle again and again before you are able to change your old habits. Someone has said, "It takes three weeks to form a new habit." But it can take longer to change some old habits. Don't be discouraged just keep going! For instance, I still find myself answering folks who ask how I am doing with some form of the word, "good."

That is why in this book's companion volume, "Living With and Loving All of God's Children," I have given you one hundred and forty-four other ways to respond to those who may ask you, "How are you doing today?"

You can read this book all the way through for entertainment. You can also pick it up on a flight, while waiting for a doctor or dentist's appointment, during your family vacation, while traveling in the back seat of your family car, or just while home relaxing. You can open it up and begin reading on any page. However, if you are truly serious about learning how to make your dreams come true and how to be an effective leader and a better employee, you will have fun putting the principles discussed herein into practice.

When you reach the end of this book, you will discover your Captain's log. You may wish to record your victories and successes there for future reference.

Summary of the Above Suggestions

A. Decide to change your life.
B. Visualize and imagine...See the new you.
C. Do not compare yourself to other people.
D. Read this book with your family or with friends.
E. Invite everyone in the group to take a turn reading one or more sub-headings as you desire.
F. Discuss what has been read.
G. Go out and practice the principle (s) taught. Do it. Get it done.
H. Don't be afraid to fail.
I. Discuss your victories and successes the next time you meet as a group.
J. Repeat the process.

How to Make Your Dreams Come True

Use Your Imagination

When we were young boys growing up in California, my brother Tommy and I loved to imagine we were the Long Ranger and Tonto. We patrolled the streets and alleyways of our neighborhood on our bicycles, looking for bad men or burglars who might creep in and catch the neighbors unawares. My bicycle with chrome fenders, became the Lone Ranger's horse, "Silver" and Tommy's bicycle became Tonto's horse, named "Scout." One day when I was perhaps seven years old and Tommy was five, we strapped on our holsters and cap guns and rode to the empty field behind our grade school. The empty and open ground the size of two football fields was covered in dry, white grass that reflected the summer sun. We decided to build a campfire in a place we had cleared off away from the tall grass. All was going well until a gust of wind blew the fire onto the dry grass.

We tried to put it out, but the fire got away from us, so we got away from the fire. We rode our bikes back to the safety of our home five houses away from our grade school. Our mother quickly deposited two little boys in the bathtub and washed the smoke off.

Our father worked at McClelland Air Force Base as a fireman who was prepared to put out the fires that might start in Air Force planes. When our father returned home after working 24 hours on the previous day, two little boys had to face the music. Mom and dad sat us down, and explained the dangers of playing with matches. That was the end of our fire-setting careers. Sorry, grade school alma mater. We didn't mean to leave your fields all charcoal black. Yes, Sacramento fire department-the Lone Ranger set that fire.

The Garden Hoe

When we were even younger, Tommy and I were each given a toy garden hoe and shovel for Christmas. Dad was in the back yard planting corn. We wanted to help. Somehow, Tommy's hoe ended up stuck in the top of my head. I calmly walked through the back porch door and into the living room with blood running down the side of my face and the hoe still stuck in the top of my head. I said, "Hey mom, get this hoe out of my head!"

There just happened to be a lady in the living room trying to sell encyclopedias to my mother. She took one look at that scene and promptly fainted dead away. My mother had to lay her down on the couch to let her recover, before she could get the hoe removed from my head and take me to the doctor to get stitched up. This is about the one-hundredth part of what my mother has done for her children.

Tommy and the Tomahawk

When I was a little older, I made my first tomahawk fashioned from wood. One afternoon when we were playing in our backyard, I decided to test my new creation. I sent it sailing across the backyard. It slid over the top of a big wooden crate Tommy was hiding behind. Tommy raised his head just as the tomahawk reached him and it caught him above his right eye.

Early the next morning when Dad and I were getting ready to go pheasant hunting, Tommy was left behind in his bed with a lump the size of a goose egg above his right eye. I felt sorry for him being left at home but I still went pheasant hunting with my Dad. I have always hoped Tommy forgave me for that goose egg above his eye and having to miss out on hunting. I hope he forgave me the way I forgave him for planting a toy hoe in the top of my head.

All of those experiences as children make me realize today, that we were being watched over and looked after by angels back then, otherwise we may not have survived childhood.

Each one of the stories you have just read were about two little boys playing "make believe" and imagining that they were: the Lone Ranger and Tonto, two farmers helping their dad to plant corn, or Indians playing with a real tomahawk.

Saturday Afternoon Movies

By the time I was eight and my brother was six, we were given permission to cross El Camino Boulevard and then follow the sidewalks to the Del Paso Theater one mile away. Every Saturday, the afternoon matinee included two double features, cartoons and a newsreel. The double features we would get to see were: Hopalong Cassidy, Gene Autry, Roy Rogers and Red Ryder.

Tommy and I loved watching those cowboy movies on Saturday afternoons. They fueled our growing imaginations even more. During one "shoot-em up" scene, we both got so excited we stood up on the movie seats and began shooting our cap guns (we had sneaked into the theater) at the bad guys. I had just taken a big bite of my Milky Way candy bar but now, in my excitement, I had swallowed that big bite of candy bar and I was choking.

I signaled Tommy to slap me on the back real hard. After two or three hard slaps that candy bar went sailing out over two or three rows of movie seats and landed on someone's head. But I could breathe again.

Our mile-long walks to the Saturday afternoon movies and then another mile long walk back home, were uneventful until on one afternoon for our walk home I decided to explorethe alleys starting behind the movie theater. All was going well until a bum jumped up from behind a row of garbage cans and scared the two of us so much that we ran all the way home.

My Home Made Bow and Arrows

I discovered a comic book that showed an Indian hiding up in a tree with a bow and arrows waiting to shoot a deer approaching below. I decided to make my own bow. It took some doing, but I managed to make a fine bow. Then I made a quiver and filled it with homemade arrows. The arrows were made from doweling just the right diameter and length. I glued on real feathers and notched the end of the arrows to fit the bowstring.

I had to test the arrows so I shot them high into the sky but when they came back down, two arrows landed in our neighbor's back yard. I didn't want to climb over his fence to get them so I decided to wait. I knew he would find them and tell my dad. I retrieved the two arrows but it was barely worth it because of the scolding from my father that followed. Many cowboy and Indian fights came from having my own bow and arrows. I still carry a scar on my left hand from and enemy arrow.

One day, my mother stopped me just as I arrived home from school and asked me to please not get mad with my little brother. He had broken my bow. It was a good bow and I was proud of it. I didn't get mad at my brother. It was an accident. I made another bow and some more homemade arrows.

By now, my imagination was growing and my ability to fashion the tools a real Indian would use or better yet, to imagine I was a real Indian was reaching epic proportions!

Our Back Yard Fort

We built a fort in our backyard with adobe bricks we made ourselves. We even made underground tunnels complete with escape hatches. We needed a way to defend our fort. I found two old tire inner tubes. I cut them up to make our own dirt clod launchers. Tommy and I made a nice pile of dirt clods. We needed a target to test our new launchers. The white stucco wall of our neighbor's detached garage was an inviting target. When we finished testing our dirt launchers the white wall of our neighbor's garage was filled with clod pelt marks.

One afternoon after a long, hard rain, we decided it would be great fun to climb up on the white picket fence surrounding our back yard and jump into the wet and soggy mud that now made up all the back yard around our fort. Tommy and I were having fun jumping into the mud when Patty, then just two years old asked to join us.

We lifted her up onto the fence top and she jumped into the mud, then disappeared. We forgot we had dug underground tunnels everywhere. Patty had jumped on top of an underground tunnel. The integrity of the tunnel, weakened by Tommy and me jumping on top of it, had collapsed. Patty sunk down into the tunnel. Tommy jumped off the fence to pull Patty out then I jumped in to pull Tommy out.

King Arthur and the Knights of the Round Table

When I was in the fifth grade my teacher, Mrs. Fish, gave me my first full-length book to read. It was all about King Arthur and the Knights of the Round Table, and the magnificent sword Excalibur. I was just ten years old then because I had skipped half of the fourth and fifth grades and I started kindergarten when I was four. When I finished reading that book, I told my brother that I would make two wooden swords so we could have sword fights.

We still needed two shields. We rode our bicycles behind the nearby Wonder Bread Bakery and looked around their dumpster and found two big pieces of waxed cardboard. With a little cutting and shaping we had our two shields. Almost magically, two little boys were wonderfully transformed into two knights from King Arthur's court.

Everything you have just read about was made from the imagination of two little boys. Nothing was without error, but everything we made to play with was more than good enough for us as youngsters. We never once thought about whether our playthings were perfect, we just used our imagination and we became cowboys and Indians, the Lone Ranger and Tonto, and knights of King Arthur's Round Table.

So if you want to make your dreams come true, stop worrying about perfection. Just get whatever it is you are dreaming about out there and into the world. Make it the best you can with what you have. Then, the world will, at least, see a manifestation of your dreams. Perfection can come later. But in reality, we are on a life-long journey striving for perfection, and we may never once reach it in this life, so do the very best you can with what you have and your dreams will begin to come true.

Make a Drawing of Your Ideas

When I was eleven, I made a drawing of what I hoped would be my first invention. My idea was to improve upon Sam Colt's famous Colt 45 by making it belt-fed to accommodate 12 to 16 rounds of .45 ACP cartridges instead of just six .45 long colt cartridges. There would no longer be any need for the cylinder holding six bullets and each shell would be ejected after it was fired.

Again, everything you have just read was about using your imagination. Never underestimate the power of your own imagination. So if you want to make your dreams come true begin by using your own best thinking.

Find Others to Help You

If you hope to make your dreams come true, it will require the help of other people. Thomas Edison discovered the filament that would become the essence of the inner light bulb. But before the bulb would be found in homes across America, a huge corporation would be needed to manufacture it and get it into American homes.

If you take time to read all of the credits that follow a major motion picture today, you may be amazed to see how many people contributed to making the idea and dream of that movie become a reality.

So if you hope to make your dreams into realities first have faith in others and learn to love others because you will need them to make your ideas and dreams reach fruition. But most important of all, have faith in yourself and learn to love yourself. So if you want to see your dreams come true, learn to love all of God's children and believe in yourself and love yourself.

Dream Big

If you want to reach your dreams, dream big. Dream for the stars and you may land on the moon but if you only reach for the roof of your house it may be difficult to get beyond the earth's atmosphere. So if you want to reach your dreams, again, reach for the stars but keep your feet planted firmly on the ground.

The world needs more dreamers not less. Without dreamers, the world and humanity would stay the same year after year, century after century. Dreamers are not afraid to fail. Dreamers know that they must fail first, to succeed. Trial and error is a way of life for a dreamer but when dreamers fail, they are also not afraid to pick themselves back up and start again.

When dreamers continue to run into brick walls and closed windows and doors, they eventually learn to walk around the obstacle and try again. Ultimately, some dreamers realize that to readjust their dreams and to even, perhaps, choose brand new dreams, will make them the happiest and serve humanity the best in the end.

Have a Back-up Plan

Unless you are Caesar with your own army crossing the Rubicon to fight the enemy and conquer or die, it is probably not a good idea to burn all your bridges behind you. Every plan is worthy of a back-up plan or a plan B. To have a change of plans and retreat is not admitting defeat, it is simply living to fight on another day.

For example, one friend wanted to be an Olympic athlete. That was a great dream but when he realized that would not be possible, he readjusted his dream to becoming a high school track coach.

Another friend wanted to be an actress

but when she found out that wasn't really what she wanted she decided to teach young girls to dance and how to have self-esteem. If your dream helps others to be better, it may turn out to be the best dream of all.

Visualize Your Dream

When I was about ten and a half years old my father helped me to get my first real job. It was an after school paper route that would earn me $30 a month. If I could get more customers, I could earn even more. I did get more customers. My Sacramento Bee paper route gave me a sense of responsibility and purpose but it was more than that. It was my first business. It allowed me to be my own boss and work for myself. I have followed that pattern all of my life.

My father taught me to save my money and to pay cash for major purchases. I first saw a picture of what I wanted in a magazine. It was something to behold. From the moment I saw the ad, I knew that one day, the Schwinn Phantom bicycle would be mine.

Boy's 26-inch Model B19

"The Phantom is the most famous balloon-tired bicycle in the world, with beautiful styling and lavish equipment. The Cantilever frame, chrome-trimmed tank, spring fork, chrome fenders with built-in "fenderlite" and genuine leather saddle make the Phantom the best bike money can buy." (From: the original ad, by Schwinn).

  The bicycle came with a front headlight and a back red reflector. It even came with a holder on the back to throw saddlebags (where I could carry newspapers). But the coolest piece of equipment it had was a built in push-button horn. I couldn't wait to own it and to purchase it with my own money, but it would take time.

  I figured if I worked for four or five months, I would have the money I needed to buy my new Schwinn Phantom bicycle. I also needed money to fuel my stamp and coin collections and to buy model airplanes and to be able to buy baseball cards. In time I had saved the $95 needed to purchase my Schwinn.

I guess I was the proudest boy in our community when I took my bicycle out for its first spin through the neighborhood. I don't remember how many times I honked the push button horn, but it was a lot

Decide What You Want and Have a Burning Desire to Get It

Before I could save enough to purchase my first car, I would need a second morning paper route, then a dishwashing job at a nearby hotel and then a job in a grocery store as a box boy. I can still remember my father driving me over to purchase the car with one of my friends. It was sitting in our driveway, all paid for, on the day I turned fifteen and a half, and was able to get my learner's permit to drive.

Give Yourself a Deadline

Give yourself a deadline. If you do not, you may never finish your plans and ideas and dreams. When Michelangelo was lying on his back supported by scaffolding and painting the Sistine Chapel, the pope reportedly walked in to look things over and asked him, "When will you make an end?" Michelangelo answered, "When it is finished." But in the real world, even creative people don't have the luxury of endless amounts of time. Magazines have deadlines. Bills have due dates.

If the director of a major motion picture takes longer to finish than the budget calls for, cost overruns can skyrocket. When that happens, history has shown that few such motion pictures ever earn enough to cover the additional cost, and those who made the film seldom get the opportunity to make another. So if you want to make your dreams come true, give yourself a due date to finish whatever your dream is, then make every effort to finish on your due date.

Overcoming Adversity and Paying Your Dues

It makes no difference if you are young or old, rich or poor, everyone will be tested by God. That is one of the reasons we came to earth. There will always be some who believe they are the only ones in the world with problems to overcome. That is just not true. There are so many others who have told me, "If I just had the other fellas troubles instead of my own." A closer examination of the other fella's problems will probably reveal the fact that his troubles are far greater than you had suspected.

I know one man who has survived not

one, but two brain surgeries to remove brain tumors. I know another who has beaten cancer for years. Both of these men are more humble and closer to God for having fought those battles. I know others who have lost their businesses or jobs and have struggled to put food on the table yet they have survived.

There are others who have lost their homes and have been cast out almost literally on the street, but they too have survived. I know a man in Arizona who woke up one morning to have his wife tell him she was leaving him and the children and yet, he and the children survived. Still countless other children have lost one or both of their parents at a young and tender age and they have survived.

What does all of this adversity tell you? Perhaps it is this, "if life gives you lemons, make lemonade." God does not test man to make him weaker but stronger. God does not give men weaknesses to make them weaker but to make them more humble. God will never give you a test you cannot pass, if you will humble yourself before God, have faith in Jesus Christ and trust in him.

I believe that before one can make their dreams come true; it is necessary to pass the various tests of life. Some call this, "paying your dues." I like to call it, "continuing to overcome adversity." For those who cannot deal with the tests and the adversity that comes before them, they seem to be cast out into the roadways of life without direction and no idea what to do next. Will you have the courage to pass your test or will you weaken and crumble?

There Will Be Bumps in the Road Along the Way

You will do well not to just be prepared but to be ready for the unexpected.

The Mountain Lion's Unexpected Appearance

One day Tommy and I headed off to the American River where I had spotted three big fish in a semi stagnant stretch of water the day before. I brought the fishing pole to catch the fish and Tommy brought his single shot 20-gauge shotgun with a modified choke to shoot the quail I had also noticed the day before. When we were about to walk out of the jungle-like river bottoms empty handed, I spied a mountain lion about 100 yards away in the open field in front of us. The mountain lion had already heard us coming.

She was standing up on her hind legs and looking right at us when I spotted her. We quickly hid behind a huge tree that was right next to us. To say we were scared out of our wits would be an understatement. We knew if that mountain lion came running after us, we would have little chance of getting away alive. If I would have had my Winchester 30-30 with me on that day, I could have made quick work of that mountain lion. But I never once fired it anywhere near where we lived. When I first purchased it, dad took me far out into the country where we could see at least 700 yards out. There was a hill for a backstop. Dad said that would be a safe place to sight in my new rifle. I think I was only able to fire it once or twice.

God Protects Us If We Do What He Asks of Us

God will protect all those who love him and keep his commandments. God will also protect all who have the potential to draw near unto him and love him and keep his commandments and bring souls unto him. We must remember, God knows the hearts of all his children.

If you separate yourself from God the moment adversity comes, you are missing the whole meaning of life! And what is the meaning of life? The answer is, "Fear God and keep his commandments, for this is the whole duty of man" (Ecclesiastes 12:13).

May I suggest that you go to your Bible and begin reading, "The Book of Job." It is all about adversity. Search out and ponder that narrative. There is more to learn there concerning man's salvation than first meets the eye.

To make your dreams come true, you will need to have a clearly defined dream or goal…

Goals and Planning

To have a goal is to have direction, stability, and purpose. Without having a goal in life, man is like a ship without a rudder, being tossed about aimlessly by the wind, and carried by the currents of life to wherever they take you. To have a goal is to have a dream. It gives you a reason to wake up in the morning. Setting small goals is a more realistic and down to earth version of your big dream.

Setting smaller goals will allow you to have little victories right away. This will allow your confidence to grow. Rome wasn't built in a day. The palaces, the aqueducts with fresh running water, the coliseum, and the cobble stone streets that carried horses and chariots across the city, were not built in one day. But before Rome was built, people had to live somewhere. The first makeshift and temporary shelters may have gone up in just a few days.

Start with what you have and work from there. Perfection comes later. You are probably not ready for perfection now anyway.

Instead of making a list of all the reasons why you can't make your dreams come true, why not start making a list of all the reasons why you can? God did not make man to fail. God made man so resilient that he is capable of overcoming every obstacle that might be placed before him.

But you must believe in yourself. You must really want your dream to come true. Then just get out there and make it happen. I love the indomitable spirit of the man who is able to say, "No matter what happens, I will not quit. I will finish my course. I will win the victory. I will keep the faith."

If you want to reach your goal, write it down. Define it. If it is a song, and all you have is the title, write it down. If it is a building, you dream of making real, draw a picture of the building. Then write down the date you will reach your goal.

Henry Ford gave us the Model T Ford. It was the first car built on an assembly line, and the first automobile Americans could afford to own, and that changed everything. When Ford encountered a problem to which he did not know the answer, he simply pressed a black button on his desk and an array of employees came running to solve the problem. We will not all have that luxury. But everyone can start with what they have, and work from there. Orville and Wilbur Wright built the first airplane to sustain flight in America in their garage, using bicycle parts.

Where There Is a Will, There Is a Way

An eleven-year old girl from my neighborhood decided she wanted to visit New York this summer and see several of her favorite Broadway Shows. She asked her grandmother to help her bake the scrumptious homemade bread for which her grandmother was famous. She went about the neighborhood selling the bread. When the dust settled, she had earned $1,600, which was more than enough to take her trip to New York. She left with a group of older friends with her family's blessing.

Do What You Are Good At and Do What You Love

Find out what you are good at doing by asking a friend to tell you. Hopefully your friend will be honest and able to tell the truth. Also, find out what you love to do. So many folks settle for just doing anything. They explain that bills must be paid, and they list many other reasons.

Those who do manage to make their dreams into realities do whatever it takes to get to where they want to be and they are willing to pay their dues. Bob Hope lived to be 100 years of age. In large part, I believe, it was because he loved entertaining people and making them laugh.

George Burns also lived to 100 years. From the (*Orlando Sentinel*,) dated, November 4, 1991, we read, "George Burns says he signed a five-year deal with the Riviera Hotel in Las Vegas-instead of 10 years-because he wasn't sure the resort would last until 2001." "They wanted to make it 10 years," but I said "What's the hurry?" the 96-year old comic said. "I told them if you're still around; we'll talk." "Why would anybody want to retire?" asked Burns.

The truly blessed find out what they do best, and what they love to do, and keep working and believing until they find success. The Bible teaches: "faith without works is dead" (James 2:20). But faith with works and endurance can make all your dreams come true!

Never Give Up

Thomas Edison had a dream and an idea as to how to make a light bulb. He implemented his plan through experimentation. He also kept records of each experiment that failed, so he would not continue making the same mistakes. Edison failed 5,000 times before he discovered exactly what filament would make the light bulb bring forth light.

To fail at something does not a failure make. But if Edison would not have had his idea and made his plan, which included keeping records of his mistakes, we may not have had the light bulb today. Leonardo Da Vinci filled his notebooks with meticulous drawings of his plans and dreams for a better world. But only a small portion of the drawings would come to fruition in his lifetime.

From the General Epistle of James we read, "Go to now, ye that say, Today or tomorrow we will go into such a city and continue there a year, and buy and sell and get gain; Whereas ye know not what shall be on the morrow, for what is your life? It is even a vapour, that appeareth for a little time, and then vanisheth away. For that ye ought to say, If the Lord will, we shall live, and do this, or that" (James 4: 13-15).

To be confident is good. But to have confidence in yourself and to be humble, and believe that God will help you if you ask for God's help, is even better. God will help you reach your goals and dreams if you ask for His help.

I like the powerful idea of some, "Let's see what the Lord has in mind." I especially like the following scriptures, "I can do all things through Christ which strengtheneth me" (Philippians 4:13). And, "Trust in the Lord with all thine heart; and lean not unto thine own understanding. In all thy ways acknowledge him, and he shall direct thy paths" (Proverbs 3:5-6).

If you do not have a goal, how do you expect to reach it? If you do not plan your life and just let life take you wherever it may, you will be like that ship without a rudder (already mentioned) carried about by the winds and currents until you end up, who knows where?

The world needs more dreamers who can make a plan and set down a goal so as to eventually make their dreams come true. To learn by trial and error, and by making mistakes, is how we all must learn, at least to some degree. Those who have all they ever wanted handed to them on a silver platter will never learn the hard lessons of life.

You may have stacks of notebooks filled with your plans and dreams, but the only ones that will count, and be recognized and acknowledged, are the ones you finish. Dreams and ideas carefully written down in note books may never be discovered until thousands of years after you are dead and gone and by then your plans and dreams may not be understood by those who discover them.

To leave your legacy behind, get your plans, goals, and dreams finished, while you are alive and breathing. But even if you should not finish all of this in your lifetime, writing such down and then passing them on to others, will allow your contribution to a better world to be seen by someone and when it is, your legacy will be assured.

Continue Learning

NASA and our astrophysicists have told us that the earth is about 4.3 billion years old and our known universe is about 13.7 billion years old. The Milky Way galaxy contains between 200 and 400 billion stars and at least 100 billion planets. The Andromeda Galaxy is made up of ONE TRILLION STARS. THAT'S TRILLION! NASA now believes there are 500 billion galaxies in our universe. (From Wikipedia, the free encyclopedia).

The astronauts who were the first men to

see an "earthrise" read from the Bible: *"In the beginning God created the heavens and the earth" (Genesis 1:1).* God could not have created all of that, unless He knew everything. But how can we obtain knowledge of heavenly things?

We find our first clue in the book of Proverbs. We read, "The fear of the Lord is the beginning of knowledge but fools despise wisdom and instruction" (Proverbs 1:7). God is suggesting that if we would acquire knowledge and then wisdom and understanding, the place to start is by fearing God. If a person fears God, that person will do what God asks him to do. Everyone should desire knowledge, wisdom and understanding. That is what everyone should want and the Lord has just told you how to get it.

There is another scripture in the book of Ecclesiastes that tells us how we can acquire all of these things, "Let us hear the conclusion of the whole matter: Fear God and keep his commandments for this is the whole duty of man" (Ecclesiastes 12:13).

By keeping God's commandments, we will be much better positioned to understand the ways of the world and to be able to solve our own problems. But here comes the good part. By keeping God's commandments, it will be easier for us to make our dreams come true because we will have a little more of God's light and understanding with which to do that. James has given us a beautiful promise, "But the wisdom that is from above is first pure, then peaceable, gentle, and easy to be entreated, full of mercy and good fruits, without partiality, and without hypocrisy" (James 3:17).

So if you want to make your dreams come true, fear God and keep his commandments.

The Heartbeat of America

The heartbeat of America when I was growing up was the music being played on the radio. Rock and roll was in its infancy and what a thing it was! DJ's announced the artist and the title of each song they played and I knew every song after just hearing three or four notes. I listened to the Hit Parade on the radio and later, American Bandstand on television.

The first song I remember hearing on the radio as a young boy was Gene Autry's, "Rudolph the Red-Nosed Reindeer." I heard the song at my grandmother's home in her living room on her radio at Christmas time. I liked the song immediately and I began to sing along with the song upon first hearing it.

"Gene Autry's recording sold 1.75 million copies its first Christmas season, eventually selling a total of 12.5 million. Cover versions included, sales exceed 150 million copies, second only to Bing Crosby's "White Christmas." (From Wikipedia, the free encyclopedia).

The next song that made a big impression on me was Patti Page's recording of "How Much Is That Doggie in the Window?" These songs preceded the advent of rock and roll but they were important because they were different than the sugary sweet songs that were being played on the radio at the time.

Although Bill Haley and His Comets' recording of ""Rock Around the Clock" is credited for getting young people to take notice of rock and roll, I never thought the song was that strong.

For me, four songs have formed the foundation of rock and roll. From these songs, the majority of rock and roll records that followed were influenced. The first of these is Chuck Berry's recording of "Maybellene." released in 1955. Not only have Chuck Berry's guitar licks to "Maybellene" and "Jonny B. Goode" been copied by almost every rock and roll guitar player who has heard those songs, Berry's guitar playing on "Maybellene" defines the sound of rock and roll. The song begins with the strong driving backbeat of great guitar licks and then the classic lyrics follow, "As I was motivatin' over the hill, I saw Maybellene in a Coupe De Ville." Chuck Berry is, without question, one of the founders of rock and roll music.

The next song I believe formed the foundation of rock and roll is Little Richard's "Tutti Frutti." Released in 1955. with its opening cry of "A-wop-bom-a-loo-mop-a-lop-bom-bom," the song makes a strong and immediate impression upon the listener.

In 2007, an eclectic panel of renowned

recording artists voted "Tutti Frutti" No. 1 on Mojo's *The Top 100 Records That Changed The World,* hailing the recording as "the sound of the birth of rock and roll." In 2010, the U.S. Library of Congress National Recording Registry added the recording to its registry, claiming the "unique vocalizing over the irresistible beat announced a new era in music" In April 2012, *Rolling Stone* magazine declared that the song "still contains what has to be considered the most inspired rock lyric ever recorded."

Elvis Presley's recording of "Hound Dog" released in 1956 is the third song I believe makes up the foundation of rock and roll. The song, "Hound Dog" was originally written by Jerry Leiber and Mike Stoller when they were just 19 years old. They wrote the song on a paper bag in about 12 minutes. The song was written to give "Big Mamma Thornton" her first hit. "It was recorded by her on August 13, 1952 in Los Angeles and released by Peacock Records in March 1953. "Hound Dog" was Thornton's only hit record, spending 14 weeks in the R&B charts, including seven weeks at #1." (From Wikipedia, the free encyclopedia).

However, it was not until Elvis Presley recorded the song and it was played on the radio in 1956 that the song became one of the foundation stones of the birth of rock and roll. The pairing of Presley and the Jordanaires provided a seamless match of flawless background harmonies with Elvis's electric vocals. (From BBC.Co.UK). The hook for Elvis's version of "Hound Dog" was D. J. Fontana's work on the snare drum at just the right moments in the song. If you go to YouTube and watch Elvis perform "Hound Dog" on the Milton Berle show you will quickly know why Elvis Presley became a star and why "Hound Dog" became a mega hit. Elvis's version of the song sold 10 million copies and it is still selling today.

The fourth song from which rock and roll music sprang in my view is Buddy Holley's recording of, "That'll Be the Day," released in May of 1957. Buddy Holley's song has more than one hook. The first is the guitar intro and the guitar playing throughout the song. You can also hear a melody and not just loud singing. Another hook is the constant repeating of the title, "That'll Be the Day."

In addition to this, Holley's vocal styling of the song was new and fresh and I can hear nuances of Buddy Holley in the early Beatle records. It is interesting to me that the first demo record the Beatle's ever made, when they called themselves the "Quarrymen" was none other than Buddy Holley's, "That'll Be the Day." "In 1958, the song was the first track ever recorded by The Quarrymen. The one and only 1958 pressing is thought to be one of the world's most valuable records, worth an estimated £100,000. Norman Petty sold the publishing rights to the Buddy Holly catalogue to Paul McCartney in 1979." (From Wikipedia, the free encyclopedia).

The are some lessons to be learned from listening to the old rock and roll songs and studying the history of rock and roll's first stars. Here are ten more ways you can make your dreams come true:

Be the First

The Beatles were the first English rock band to reach America and they started the English invasion. Their song, "I Want to Hold Your Hand" reached number one and sold one million records two days after it was first heard all across America on February the 4th 1964. So they were the first English band to have a number one record in America. The Beatles were the first English band to be seen, on the Ed Sullivan show on February the 9th 1964. (www.History.com)

So if you hope to make your dreams come true, do whatever it takes to be the first.

Have a Follow Up Ready to Go

If you do not, you could be a one hit wonder. The Beatles had recorded the following list of songs before arriving as a group in America to play the Ed Sullivan show on February 9, 1964:

"Love Me Do" / "P.S. I Love You" released, and played on Radio Luxembourg, October 5, 1962; "Love Me Do" enters the UK singles chart, October 26, 1962; "Please Please Me" / "Ask Me Why" released, January 11, 1963; "From Me to

You" / "Thank You Girl" released, April 11, 1963; "My Bonnie" released July 12, 1963; "Twist and Shout" released, July 12, 1963; "She Loves You"/ "I'll Get You" released, August 23, 1963; "I Want to Hold Your Hand" / "This Boy" released, November 29, 1963; "Roll Over Beethoven"/ "Please Mr. Postman" released, December 9, 1963; "I Want to Hold Your Hand"/ "I Saw Her Standing There" released, December 26, 1963; "Sweet Georgia Brown" / "Nobody's Child" released, January 31, 1964; "Introducing The Beatles" Album released, January 10, 1964; "Meet the Beatles" Album released, January 20, 1964; "All My Loving" released, February 07, 1964. (From Wikipedia, the free encyclopedia).

The Beatles had the following number one records in the UK before coming to America:

"From Me to You" number one, 02 May 1963 for seven weeks. "She Loves You" number one, 12 September 1963 for four weeks; number one again on 26 November 1963 for two weeks; "I Want to Hold Your Hand" number one, 12 December 1963 for five weeks.

"The Beatles song "She Loves You" became the best-selling single of all time in 1963, a record that held until 1977 when band member Paul McCartney's new band, Wings, surpassed it with "Mull of Kintyre." "She Loves You' was the best-selling song of the decade and one of fourteen songs believed to have sold over one million copies in the 1960's." (From

Wikipedia, the free encyclopedia).

These are the UK Singles released before February 9, 1964 when the Beatles played the Ed Sullivan show:

"My Bonnie" 5 January 1962; "Love Me Do" 5 October 1962; "Please Please Me" 11 January 1963; "From Me to You" 11 April 1963; "She Loves You" 23 August 1963; "I Want to Hold Your Hand" 23 November 1963. (From Wikipedia, the free encyclopedia).

These are the US singles released before February 9, 1964:

"My Bonnie" 23 April 1962; "Please Please Me" 25 February 1963; "From Me to You" 27 May 1963; "She Loves You" 25 January 1964. (From Wikipedia, the free encyclopedia).

So if you want to make your dreams come true, have a follow up to whatever your dream may be prepared and waiting.

Be Original, Be Different, Be Unusual

When Elvis Presley was first seen on the Ed Sullivan show with his long sideburns and wavy hair, his hairstyle was considered rebellious. When Elvis began to shake his hips that was considered obscene by some. Elvis Presley would be thought of as tame if he were discovered today. But Elvis was an original. He was different and unusual when he first hit the scene.

So if you want to be a success with your own dreams, be an original. Be different and unusual.

Find Something or Someone to Inspire You

When Buddy Holley went to the movies one afternoon and saw John Ford's motion picture "The Searchers" he noticed that John Wayne's character said, "That'll be the day" several times. That inspired Buddy Holley to go home and write his song, "That'll Be the Day."

"Paul Anka's hit song, "Diana" was reportedly inspired by a high school friend of Anka's named Diana Ayou. In an interview with NPR's Terry Gross in 2005, Anka stated that it was inspired by a girl at his church whom he hardly knew. The song reached number one in both America and the UK and has reportedly sold more than nine million copies." (From Wikipedia, the free encyclopedia).

Speaking of Paul Anka, Buddy Holley asked him to write a song for him. Apparently, he forgot to write the song and when he was reminded of Buddy's request, he wrote, "It Doesn't Matter Anymore" in a matter of minutes and gave it to Buddy Holley. When he learned Buddy Holley was killed in a plane crash, just months later, Paul Anka gave the rights to his song to Buddy Holley's widow. That act of kindness speaks volumes of Paul Anka's character.

So if you want to make your dreams come true, find something or someone to inspire you.

The Combination of Two or More Great Things Can Often Make Another Great Thing

Peanut butter and jelly sandwiches are an example of three great things, peanut butter, jelly and bread. Rock and roll is a combination of the following genres of music: blues, rhythm and blues, boogie-woogie, gospel and country music. Chuck Berry called his hit song, "Maybelene," "just a little country song."

Keep It Simple

If you listen to Elvis Presley's recording of "Hound Dog" you will discover that it is not deceptively simple, it is just plain simple. It is not complicated at all but very easy to remember upon hearing it just one time. I love the old rock and roll songs because they began and ended in just a few seconds over two minutes. That means the song had just over two minutes to get your attention and grab you and leave a lasting and favorable impression on you.

So if you want to make your dream come true, keep it simple. If your dream tends towards being long, and complex try breaking it up into smaller parts. Remember the attention span of the average human is not infinitely long.

Have a Hook

Again, one of the best hooks of any rock and roll song ever written is Little Richard's opening to "Tutti Frutti" when he yells, 'A-wop-bom-a-loo-mop-a-lomp-bom-bom!"

Does your big dream have a hook? If it does not, go out and find yourself one if you hope to make your dream come true.

Repeat Yourself

When you listen to Gene Autry's recording of Rudolph the Red-Nosed Reindeer, you will notice that the song does not have a traditional bridge with a different melody and different lyrics. The song simply continues to use its one and only melody line, with instruments for the bridge and then the song continues with its only melody line and lyrics until it ends. We should all constantly remind ourselves to stay on point.

When I was growing up in California, if a record was played on the radio every half an hour, kids would begin to listen for it and it was sure to become a hit. When a new record was played every 15 minutes, it would almost certainly become a mega hit.

So if you want to make your dream come true, repeat yourself again and again and stay on point.

Exposure to the Masses Is Needed to Succeed Big

Back in the days of early rock and roll there was only the radio. The radio show "Your Hit Parade" was a big help in making songs hit records early on. When television was introduced, rock and roll acts could be seen on the Milton Berle show; The Ed Sullivan Show; and later, Dick Clark's American Bandstand. It was no coincidence that Ricky Nelson played each of his new records on "The Ozzie and Harriet" television show. This exposure allowed his fans to both see and hear him perform his latest songs and helped them to become hit records.

Everything after the Beatles' first appearance on the Ed Sullivan show in early February of 1964 is history. But there is a little history that has recently come to light. George Harrison visited his sister Louise in Benton, Illinois on September 16 of 1963 and brought a copy of the Beatles' record, "She Loves You" with him. He was able to get a local DJ to play the record on the radio then. Even before that, George's sister had a copy of "From Me To You" sent to her by their mother. George's sister took the record to WFRX-AM radio station in West Frankfort, Il. The record was played by DJ Marcia Raubach in June of 1963. (The Beatles Bible, Monday 16 September 1963).

Playing the Beatles' records on the radio

in West Frankfort, Illinois was a good idea. The town however, had a population of just 4,000 at the time and the number of people who actually heard the two records played was limited, at best.

Near worldwide exposure today can be achieved by getting your dream, whatever it may be, on the internet. To achieve success, constant exposure is vital. The presidential candidates of 2016 are constantly in the media. I have seen as many as seven posts on Yahoo's news page in one single day from one candidate and not a day goes by that most of those seeking the presidency are all over the media. By this constant exposure they are on everyone's mind often.

You may wish to consider every means available to you to get your dream out there and in front of your potential audience. Consider setting up your own professional web site and blog. If one is good, two or three will be better. You may even consider starting your own internet television show.

It seems almost every major corporation in America is now using social media such as Face Book and Twitter. My favorite site for exposure is "YouTube." You may not be able to afford to incorporate these avenues of advertising and exposure at first, so start by doing what you can early. Get your name or the name of your product or company out there early and keep your exposure constantly in front of the public eye. Once you have achieved some success keep up your constant exposure by putting your own ads and posts on the internet. When the news media pick you up, you will then be getting free advertising and that is what you want. Remember, exposure is good but overexposure will almost certainly assure your success.

Find and Hire the Best Professionals to Help You

Colonel Tom Parker found Elvis Presley and became his manager. Elvis found the Jordanaires and they became the back-up group in most of his recording sessions and helped him to make great records.

Brian Epstein became the Beatles' 'manager. The legendary Sir George Martin found the Beatles and signed them to their first recording contract. Paul McCartney has just acknowledged George Martin as the "fifth Beatle." I do not believe the Beatles could have made the records they did back then without George Martin as their brilliant producer.

So when you are ready, if you hope to make great records or to make whatever your dream is great, be certain to find yourself the best possible professionals to help you.

School Days

When I was in grade school, we began the day by reciting, "The Pledge of Allegiance." We also had air raid drills from time to time.

When I began the seventh grade, my favorite clothes to wear were blue denim Levis, a white T-shirt, a brown leather jacket, and brown leather shoes with steel horseshoe taps. When I got up a good running start, I could slide for 12 feet or more on the school's cement sidewalks. Sometimes sparks would fly. I wore my hair in a flat top boogie then, used Brylcreem for my hair and brushed my teeth with Ipana toothpaste.

Historical Events That Changed the World

I remember, "Sputnik," the first satellite the Russians sent into space on October 4, 1957. Yuri Gagarin, a Russian cosmonaut, became the first human to journey into outer space when his Vostok spacecraft completed an orbit of the Earth on April 12, 1961. (From Wikipedia, the free encyclopedia). The Russians were leading the space race in 1961.

On May 25, 1961, President Kennedy promised to send a man to the moon by the end of the decade. I was in graduate school and on my way to class during the summer of 1969 when I stopped in front of a television set to watch Neil Armstrong take the first step on the moon and to hear him say, "That's one small step for man and one giant leap for mankind."

On October 6, 1961 President Kennedy urged Americans to build bomb shelters. Some people began building fallout shelters before that, although no one in our neighborhood did that I was aware of then. The height of the cold war scare began on the day President Kennedy announced the Cuban Missile Crisis, on October 16, 1962, which lasted until October 28, 1962. Nevertheless, the cold war between the United States and Russia lasted from 1947 at the end of World War II until the dissolution of the Soviet Union on December 26, 1991. (From Daily Knowledge, November 13, 2013).

What can be learned from these events in history that changed the world? First, it would seem that it sometimes takes another nation to beat you to the punch before you can convince the powers that be to get into the competition. Next, weapons that will ultimately destroy the world never were the answer to lasting peace.

How can young people apply this to achieving success in today's world? Continue to strive to be the first to see your dreams become realities and follow the teaching of the Savior of the world, which he so eloquently taught and are perhaps best summed up with, "thou shalt love thy neighbor as thyself." (Mark 12:31).

America's Love Affair with the Automobile

By the time I was ready for my first car, Americans had already had a long lasting love affair with the automobile. My father's first car was a Model T Ford. He told me, it would make it up the steep driveways of Placer county and Lake Tahoe better in reverse than in the forward gears.

My first car was a customized 1952 Mercury painted a beautiful shade of maroon. I loved that car because it gave me a sense of freedom and independence that every teen-age boy hopes for. The car had a trunk that could open and close automatically by activating a toggle switch under the dash. It was equipped with an air scoop on the hood, push button doors and it was lowered in front to the six-inch legal limit. I added lakes pipes, and scavenger pipes.

I eventually purchased chrome Spinner hubcaps, Baby Moon and Peak Moon hubcaps, so I could change the look of the car often.

One of the initial things I did with my first car was to take my high school girl friend driving up and down the hills of Fair Oaks. I decided to pull over and give her a driving lesson since she didn't know how to drive. I sat close to be able to grab the steering wheel but she did a good job even though the car was a stick shift.

Saturday night was drive-in movie night and our senior class had our own row to park, it was row thirteen. On one particular night, the car behind us signaled me to pull over before we entered the drive-in movie and reached the ticket booth. Two of the kids in the car wanted to hide in my trunk that opened and closed with the touch of a toggle switch under my dash.

When we reached the ticket booth, I paid for my date and myself but the car behind us tapped our back bumper with their front bumper and one of the girls in the trunk screamed. I quickly drove ahead and parked the car. A man in a white trench coat burst out of the ticket booth and started running after us.

I managed to get everyone out of the trunk and we all outran the man in the long white coat as he chased us all over the drive-in. We finally found another car to hide in and watched most of the movie. I decided we had better leave before the movie was over because I suspected the theater employee would be waiting for us near the exit, at the end of the movie. Although we escaped unscathed, that wasn't the smartest thing I did as a high school student.

My Second Car

My second car was a customized 1956 Ford. I painted the car a beautiful Cadillac blue green and added Chrome wheels with "knock offs." I owned it just in time to drive it to my first college classes when I was 17. Even though gasoline was only 23 to 27 cents a gallon back then, I only earned $1.55 an hour working at the local grocery store.

No one was counting gas mileage at the time but I knew it was 10 miles one way to my high school, and about the same to college, four miles to the drive-in movies and eight miles to down town Sacramento and Mel's Drive-In. I knew it would take three dollars of gas to drive down town and cruise J Street for an hour or two and then hit Mel's Drive-In for a hamburger and a milk shake for another hour or more and still have enough gas left to get back home.

My 1956 Ford was more dependable than my first car that used to suffer from vapor lock in the hot summer weather. I took my second car to Lake Tahoe to spend the weekend with a girl friend, and then to the Bay area and to Guerneville over 100 miles away. There were many Friday nights spent cruising downtown Sacramento's J street for hours and then stopping at Mel's Drive-in hoping to be able to park on the front row so that every car that drove by could see your car.

There were no cell phones in those days, no texting, face book or twitter, so when we wanted to meet someone in the car next to us, we would just stick our heads out the window and say hello and ask what school they went to.

One night while driving out of Mel's Drive-In we all noticed another car, who's driver decided to play chicken with a slow moving freight train about a block away. The car managed to stop in time to avoid hitting the train but the front bumper was snagged by the train's engine. The train lifted the car straight up in the air and dragged it down the tracks for almost 100 yards before it stopped. No one was hurt but that was about the dumbest thing any of us saw happen back then.

My girl friend and I decided to drive to San Francisco one weekend and have a nice dinner at Fisherman's Wharf. She let me drive her car. It was a red, convertible 1963 Austin Healey Sprite. On the way back home, the left front tire hit something on the freeway from the far left lane and the car spun out of control making a complete 180 degree turn, crossing two lanes and miraculously missing other approaching cars, before I could correct it and stop the car on the far right side of the freeway.

On another afternoon I drove my younger brother and his friend with me to downtown Sacramento in my 1956 Ford. I had removed the back bumper because I had just painted the undercarriage white. I wanted to check out one of the customized car shops. On the way back home, a lady in an old Buick slammed into the back of our car. She claimed her brakes went out.

Even though I could see her coming at us, there was nothing I could do to get out of her way in time, though I tried. My brother's friend was knocked onto the road. I scrambled out of the car to help him and get him back into the front seat of the car. He already had his arm in a cast and he was known to have brittle, very easily broken bones but somehow we all escaped without injury.

You have just read three stories about the dangers that can accompany driving. One was a story of a driver doing something stupid but the other stories demonstrate that there will be times unknown to you when something will happen when you are driving for which you have no control. My neighbor just told me that he was driven off the road by an 18-wheeler not long ago, from which he suffered several serious injuries yet he survived. However, when the incident occurred there was nothing he could do to prevent it.

So always be careful to look out for the other drivers on the road. Drive defensively.

Speeding While Driving Kills

Those reading this of all ages have no doubt, heard many stories about the dangers of speeding. Before we could graduate from Driver's Ed in high school we had to watch a movie showing many graphic car crashes which were the after effects of speeding while driving. One of my uncle's was killed when he drove his 1955 Chevy into an oak tree because he was speeding on a country road when I was just 14. There are probably few neighborhoods that do not have someone living there who knows about someone who has been injured or killed because someone was speeding while driving.

Here are some statistics that may cause you to drive more defensively and begin to watch how fast you are traveling while driving on the freeways: The stopping distance for a vehicle traveling 60 mph is typically 120 to 140 feet. The average length of a pickup truck is 17 feet. That is 8.235 car lengths to stop. When you are traveling 80 miles per hour it will take 360 feet to stop. That's 21.176 car lengths or 357 feet. That's longer than the length of a football field!

This gives you a good reason not to follow too close or tailgate on the freeway.

Texting While Driving Also Kills

A cell phone can be useful and perhaps save a life should an emergency arise. However, the use of cell phones while driving, is known to cause injuries and even death.

In 2013 this article appeared: "Texting while driving is now the leading cause of death among teenagers–surpassing drinking and driving." (From a study by Cohen Children's Medical Center). A second article appeared the same year: "As of May 8, 2013, texting while driving is now the leading cause of death for teen drivers" (From, www. newsday.com). The Center in New Hyde Park estimates more than 3,000 annual teen deaths from cell phone use while driving.

That amounts to an average of nine deaths each day! Those numbers are thought to be very low because of the lack of accurate records being kept.

Texting While Driving Can Cost You $10,000 and One Year in Jail

That is the penalty if you are caught texting while driving in Alaska. The fine in Utah is $750. (From State legislatures, local media reports, Mother Jones).

Although the fine for texting while driving in California is only $20, the lowest in the nation, if you are caught in Los Angeles there will be surcharges driving the fine up to $159, and you will almost certainly see your car insurance rate rise as well. (Statistics from: Techlicious, Fox Van Allen, October 25, 2013).

"At age 19, Reggie Shaw was texting while driving and killed two men in Utah. "I texted all the time when I drove. It's something I did almost every time I got behind the wheel," he told *Here & Now*'s Robin Young. "I thought that it was safe," he said. Shaw went to jail for 30 days, and did community service. He also spoke to Utah lawmakers, to get them to pass one of the toughest laws against texting and driving in the country.

"I explained to them that this is a serious problem that this is as dangerous as anything you can do behind the wheel," he said. "A law is going to prevent families from losing their loved ones. People don't have to go through what I've put people through." Under Utah's new law, offenders face up to 15 years in prison.
(From Here & Now, July 11, 2012).

To watch a ""must see" video of the young man's story just mentioned, go to YouTube and type in:

Zero Fatalities: Reggie Shaw's Story

(Used by permission from the Utah Highway Patrol public information officer, Sgt. Todd Royce, February 2016).

There have already been more than 1,030 deaths in America caused by texting while driving, in just the first two months of 2016. (From United States of America REALTIME Current Death Toll). While that number may not seem to be that high, it still represents more than 17 fatalities per day and should that trend continue, there could be more than 6,000 fatalities from texting while driving by the year's end.

You can be the one to see to it that something is done to prevent so many deaths caused while some are still driving and using a cell phone to text with. You can set the example for others to follow. You can remind your mom and dad to turn off their cell phones while you are in the car and they are driving.

You have a choice. Please choose to turn off your cell phone while driving. Should you forget to do that, wait to drive off of the freeway or main roads, and find a safe place to park, before using your cell phone. Driving responsibly with a cell phone is just one more way you can make this a better world in which to live. In this case you will be saving human lives.

Some Cautions and Warnings

Take Responsibility for Your Mistakes

The biggest age-related problem with young men and women in high school seems to go under the radar not undetected, but unsolved. I asked one of my neighbors, who is a high school administrator in Utah what was the biggest problem he faced with high-school aged young people. He said it was when students did not take responsibility for their violations. He noted that catching them when they were truant or committing any infraction was easy enough, but getting them to acknowledge their mistakes and face up to punishment was not just difficult but in some cases, almost impossible.

He mentioned one instance when the parent demanded that her son be allowed to graduate even though he had been caught and the punishment clearly required him to be held back, and not to graduate. What was the parent's justification? She said, "My son is justified because every one else is doing it and they just haven't been caught." My neighbor said he saw the same problem over and over again when he was a high school principal in California.

When I inquired of another friend as to what was the biggest problem he faced raising his children, he was quick to answer, that when one of them does something wrong, they inevitably say, "he or she did it first." Thus, they justify themselves in doing the same thing and getting away with it because after all, their brother or sister just did it first. When I was in grade school and children were caught arguing or fighting, they would always say, "he or she started it." Children back then thought that doing such would take the blame off of them and allow them to get away with whatever it was they were doing that might be wrong.

  Unfortunately, life does not work that way. We all have to face the consequences for what we do that is right and for what we do that is wrong. The best time to learn this is when one is young. Teaching true principles to children falls upon the shoulders of parents.

  Here are some time tested ways parents can teach their children that each of us is responsible for his or her mistakes: When I joined the Civil Air Patrol, I was taught to say, "No excuse sir." Saying such taught us that we could not pass the blame onto someone else or come up with any lame excuse when we made a mistake. We learned that we alone were responsible for our mistakes.

  When I was in basic training in the Army, we quickly learned one of the often used forms of discipline was doing 10 or more push-ups. The Drill sergeant would yell out, "Get down and give me 10."

This is an effective way of teaching that there are consequences for making mistakes. Don't forget to also reward success. If all you do is to discipline children or young adults when they make mistakes, you are only seeing half of the picture and you are only teaching half of what must be taught. You must also be careful to reward success. Doing such will reinforce the desire to make good choices. Children and young people must be made to feel good about doing the right thing.

An effective way to do this is to first ask children what it is they would like to receive as their reward for making a certain number of good choices or in other words, doing the right thing for a pre-determined length of time such as one week.

You might suggest that they may choose to receive a coloring book with crayons or new magic markers or watercolors of their choice. Another idea could be a bike ride to the park where the family will have a picnic together or the children may give you other ideas for their reward. You may choose to have weekly rewards, monthly rewards and even a reward at the end of each year.

The reward for a year of good choices would be more substantial such as a trip to Disneyland for example. Be sure to discuss the discipline to be administered for mistakes such as 10 or 20 push-ups for example and the rewards to be given for good choices with the children and get them to agree. You may even wish to have them sign and date an agreement written on parchment paper and then keep the paper displayed on the kitchen wall.

Then be certain to deliver the promised reward or discipline. The idea is to focus on the rewards and not the discipline but to allow children to feel good about acknowledging their mistakes. When they agree in advance to do 10 push-ups and demonstrate that they can do that, at that point you are still only half finished with what is being taught. When the parent says, "Stand at attention sir or ma'am" and then asks, "have you done something wrong?" Be sure and wait for the child to answer and acknowledge their mistake in their own words.

If you fail to do that, you are not teaching the child that they are responsible for their mistakes. Unless they acknowledge they have made a mistake in their own words, they will never learn that they are responsible for their mistakes.

Now, the parent can say, "Get down and give me 10 sir or ma'am." When the child has completed the 10 push-ups now you can say, "Come to attention sir or ma'am." Now, comes the most important part of all. Now be certain to tell the child, "excellent work," "outstanding." "I'm proud of you for admitting your mistake and paying the consequences."

Now you may say, "At ease, sir or ma'am. As you were." You can explain to the child that, "as you were" means to resume their play or whatever it was they were doing. Now the discipline is over, it has been quick and to the point. The child has learned that there are consequences for making mistakes but the discipline is not severe. The child already knows what to expect because they have been told what to expect in advance and they have agreed to the conditions by signing and dating a parchment that has been placed in a prominent place in the kitchen.

Please remember the importance of praising another.

> A teaspoon of praise
> at the right instant
> is the
> final ingredient
> to
> the greatest recipe
> for success.

When I was under my parachute that was caught in an updraft, during Airborne Training, I ceased to fall down to the ground with the hundreds of soldiers all around me. The updraft caused my parachute to defy gravity for a short time. I was suspended in mid-air. That gave me a moment to reflect on eternal things. I realized then that I was responsible for my life, for the good or bad decisions that I made, and I alone would one day have to answer God for them. I would not be able to say, when the "day of judgment" came, "he or she did it first," or "this or that person made me do it."

When I was asked to be the platoon sergeant in both basic and advanced infantry training, I understood that I was responsible for the 54 men in my platoon. I would have to wake up a half an hour earlier than they did to make sure they were all awake and ready for that day's training whether the schedule posted on the wall said, training would begin at 4:30 AM or 5 AM. Even though I was the platoon sergeant, there was no favoritism shown to me as far as making mistakes were concerned. All soldiers training in our platoon were treated equally when it came to discipline being enforced. When I made a mistake I also suffered the consequences.

Two people walked by me yesterday and one of them said to the other, "That's someone else's problem." I couldn't help wonder how many other people would say that before that particular problem was taken care of. If everyone simply said, "That's someone else's problem" each time a problem arose, no problem would ever get solved!

President Teddy Roosevelt used to say, "The buck stops here," referring to the completion of the Panama Canal. He was telling the public that he was going to finish the Canal with or without any support. (From Yahoo answers).

Don't Interrupt When Others Speak to You

One day at school, Jane's friend took her aside and said, "Jane if you will promise not to get mad and upset with me, I will tell you something you are doing that if you can stop, you will be more popular at school and you will have more friends." Jane agreed, and her friend told her that if she could stop interrupting people when they were speaking to her, that would make all the difference.

Jane asked her friend how she could do that. Her friend suggested that she pay her a quarter for every time she interrupted people. She said the money would be saved and it could go to her favorite charity when the experiment ended. Jane went to her local bank and purchased a roll of quarters.

On the following day, the experiment began. By the end of the first day, Jane had paid her friend 17 quarters. But by the end of the second day it was only ten and by the end of the first week, it was only seven. By the end of three weeks, Jane only had to pay her friend two quarters. And she was more popular at school and she did have more friends.

The habits we have formed have taken a lifetime to get there. We cannot expect to form new habits in just a day or even in three weeks.

Keep at it. Don't get discouraged. I promise you, if you do, you will win in the end.

Don't Dominate the Conversation

I have heard a story of one young lady who sabotaged receiving her own engagement ring because she would not stop talking. Since her suitor was raised with manners and would not interrupt her, he was unable to get a word in edgewise when he wanted to present the engagement ring to this young lady. After two attempts of trying to ask for her hand in marriage, he gave up and found someone else.

So if you want life to be more kind to you, let the person you are talking with get a word in edgewise. Don't dominate the conversation.

You Can Learn to Not Get Angry

One young man told me that when he was in kindergarten playing at recess, someone pushed him, so he took off his belt and held it up. He did not whack anyone with his belt, he just held it up but one of his teachers saw him and she told the principal and the principal called his father. That put an end to his taking off his belt.

A grown woman told me that when she was in grade school someone pushed her and so she pushed that person back. She wasn't happy about doing that back then and she could still remember it all those years later. The problem with getting angry is that anger can lead to pushing and shoving, that can lead to hitting, and hitting can lead to a knock-down drag-out fight.

There are some things you can do to help you to not get angry: Decide in advance. When you can tell you are about to get angry, stop and say, "I will not get angry three times." When you feel you are about to get angry, count to ten slowly, like this: "One and two and three and four and, two and three and four and five and," and so on, until you reach the number ten. Doing this; will allow you to simmer down and settle yourself. When you can tell you are about to get angry, use your sense of humor to laugh, not at the person with whom you are angry but at yourself. Say these words, which you can commit to memory:

>Whenever I get angry
>I'm just a big buffoon.
>But if I can stop myself
>from getting angry-
>I can make it
>to the moon.

Don't Be a Complainer

Grumpy Nelly
and
Gloomy McFrown

Grumpy Nelly
and Gloomy McFrown
complained about everything
 in their little town.
According to them,
nothing was right with the world
and everything was wrong.

Only trouble is,
after awhile
everyone in town
moved away
from Grumpy Nellie
 and Gloomy McFrown.
They wanted to get as far away
from them as they could get.
They had had
quite enough
of listening to them complain.

So grumpy Nelly
and Gloomy McFrown
were left alone
in their sleepy little town
to complain to each other
to their heart's content.

Isn't it interesting how one person can wake up every morning and say, "My life and this world just keep getting worse and worse every day?" But another person wakes up to say, "My life and this world just keep getting better and better every day." How can that be?

It's the same world folks. It just depends on how you look at it. I wonder if the people who are constantly complaining realize how often they complain, and how their negative "take" on everything effects those who may be subjected to spend time around them for long hours, as in a work place?

Perhaps more importantly, I wonder if those who are always complaining realize why they are unhappy and have few if any friends. Everyone deserves to be happy and to have friends and one way to do that is to be grateful for everything in this wonderful world of ours.

Some folks spend so much time complaining about anything and everything that one can almost see a visible dark cloud around them. Trying to talk to them is almost like trying to drive through fog. I did drive through thick fog once on Interstate 5 in southern California. It was nothing but "start and stop," trying not to touch the back bumper of the car in front of me for many minutes and many miles.

Some believe that if they could just change their location their circumstances would then change. Although moving from a small town in any location to a big city could possibly give a person more opportunities for employment in their chosen line of work, changing ones location will not change ones attitude.

Someone has said, "Your attitude determines your altitude," and it can be possible for your attitude to determine how high you rise in any endeavor. If you were a complainer in your small town, you will still complain when you relocate to a big city.

Albert Einstein said, "Insanity is doing the same thing over and over and expecting different results." Don't just change your location, change your whole perspective from being negative to being positive and hopeful about everything. Start saying and believing, "It could happen." Then go out and make it happen. And here is a description of how you can do just that:

One of God's most loved creations is none other than the common, ordinary dog. This affable creature is so endeared to the hearts of men and women the world over that he has become known as, "man's best friend."

It is as if dogs are saying, "I'll be your friend, I don't need much, just an occasional meal. I won't ever complain because I haven't been given a voice but I will come to greet you every time you come home from work and I'll smile and snuggle up against you. I'll be sad when you leave but I'll be so excited to see you when you return, I'll almost jump out of my skin."

How is it possible that something as simple, and innocent yet loveable as a common ordinary dog could melt the heart of the crustiest most hardened, grumpy and complaining soul? A miracle you say, yes perhaps, but that's what happens when we forget about ourselves and begin to care about something or someone else. That caring eventually turns into love and when one loves another, that love changes a man or a woman's heart. Just look into the eyes of an innocent and loving little doggie and feel the love. Now, feel the love growing inside of you. That is the miracle!

So if you want to shed the old crusty, complaining you and trade that person in for the new you, go out and find yourself a companion who will allow you to say, "you make me want to be a better, man or woman."

If you have not been able to find that person yet, go out and find yourself your own version of man's best friend and watch the old grumpy you become the new, kind and loving you.

Making Decisions

By the time you become a teenager, you will be faced with making decisions. How will you know how to make the right choice? Some may say, trust your instincts. That is good advice. And yet, there is an even better way. God has placed the light of Christ inside of each of you.

That light which some call your conscience allows you to know the difference between right and wrong. Learn to follow that light and you will do well. You will also do well to use your common sense.

Common Sense

You know what common sense is, don't you? It's that stuff that is so common, everyone is supposed to have a little of it. Sometimes we have to make a judgment call using life experience and common sense. For example, one of my friends works in a store that sells the things homeowners often purchase. One shopper recently asked him for help to buy gas to be able to get to their destination out of state.

My friend said he had the idea to ask this person to follow him to the nearest gas station. While there, he filled that person's tank with gas. Another friend and I stopped to help a gentleman sitting on a street corner with a sign asking for help. I got out of the car and walked up to him, visited with him for a few minutes, then left him with the amount of funds I thought would be helpful.

Interestingly, the very next week, we saw this same gentleman sitting at the same corner asking for help, when a much younger man walked by asking a few people for help. The younger person approached the older man and asked him if he could spare just enough change that he might buy himself a drink at the nearby gas station.

What do you think happened next? The older man not only refused to help after we had just helped him, but actually got up out of his comfortable sitting position and easily walked away from the young man. Thus, the older man revealed himself to be just another seasoned and deceptive panhandler. This was his full time job. Yet he would not help another less fortunate person who only asked for enough change to buy a drink.

Be "Kind to Dinosaurs and Humans Too"

A certain person said to me not long ago, "That man's breath is bad and I mean real bad." I didn't think much of it until someone breathed into my face. That man's breath could have killed a dinosaur 30 yards away! Warning: when working in close proximity of other humans, please insert a breath mint into thy mouth. If you do not, that which you breath into another poor soul's face could cause permanent injury or at the very least-temporary disorientation! So, f you don't want to be thought of as *Pepe La Pue,* always carry, use, and share, breath mints when you know you will be breathing close to other humans.

For those who may not remember, *Pepe La Pue* was not a mouse or a duck like Mickey Mouse or Donald Duck, he was not a frog or a pig like Kermit the Frog or *Miss Piggy*, he was not even a squirrel or a Moose like Rocky and Bullwinkle. *Pepe La Pue,* although a loveable cartoon character, was unfortunately, a skunk.

Breath mints are sometimes not enough, if you want clean fresh breath. Begin by using mouthwash, then, brush your teeth. Flossing is helpful. Bacteria not only accumulates around your teeth and gums, but also on your tongue. Brush your tongue with toothpaste or use a tongue scraper. Adding parsley to a salad or juicing it is also effective for clean breath.

When you keep your tongue clean, you will be better able to taste your food. But best of all, it will be easier for people to get close to you.

Tolerate Insensitive People

Lend a hand when you can. Next time you find yourself standing in a line in front of a lady who gets a call on her cell phone and proceeds to talk in your ear and reveal her life story to you and all who are standing nearby, remember that although you might like to see this person temporarily on another planet, she still has the right to live here with you.

Next time you are on an airplane sitting in front of three young children who will not settle down and stop yelling and bouncing around for the entire flight, remember, the seats they are sitting in are not ejection seats and you do not get to push the ejection button. You do have the right to place earplugs in your ears and grin and bear it.

Next time you are sitting next to a young mother with her newborn babe in her arms on a long airplane flight, you have the right to offer to let the infant sit on your lap and I promise you the child will calm down. And even if there is a big wet spot on your brand new suit pants at the end of the flight, the young mother will be grateful and you will probably feel good about helping her too.

For Young Girls

It is probably not a good idea to yell at the top of your lungs with a blood-curdling scream that could wake up the dead, in the close proximity of gown-ups. You may cause your grandpa to have a heart attack or short circuit the hearing aid of your grandmother.

If you ever decide to do that, tell your dad first. He may take you to the top of Mt. Kilimanjaro, or another high mountain closer by. While there, once your dad puts in three sets of earplugs, you could scream to your heart's desire.

Who knows, the astronauts now orbiting the earth in the Space Shuttle, may hear you.

For Young Boys and Girls

It may not be wise to teach your dog to wake your father by chewing up his pillow and slobbering all over him. Should that happen on a morning when dear old dad was planning on sleeping in, you and Fido may both end up in the proverbial "dog house."

Learning Leadership Skills

Ask for God's Help

Not everyone knows there is a God. Not everyone has found God. Not everyone believes in God. But if you will begin to believe in God and ask for God's help to make your dreams come true, God will help you. God made you, He knows you and He also knows what will ultimately make you happy. Interestingly, it usually seems that which will make us the happiest involves caring for others and serving others.

The Bible says, "Ask and it shall be given you, seek and you shall find, knock and it shall be opened unto you" (Matthew 7:7). God will answer all of your prayers and questions if you will ask him.

I promise you that if you will lift others up and make others better, and treat people with love and respect, God will bless you with more peace of mind and confidence than you have ever known before.

If you are already nine or ten years old you are probably thinking about what you would like to be when you grow up. Learning great leadership skills will help you to be a success in whatever field of endeavor you choose for your life's work. Here is the beginning of some leadership principles that may help you:

Children Are the Future of the World

A two-year old child is not too young to learn great leadership skills. I was just invited to a Christmas Eve celebration. Part of the evening's program, included the host family's six children each taking their turn entertaining those in attendance.

When it was a two year old girl's turn to entertain us, she ran up to the piano bench, seated herself, and began singing and playing her song for everyone. The piano notes were incorrect; the song she sang was hit and miss; but nevertheless most delightful and everyone responded with thunderous applause whereupon the little girl ran gleefully to the loving arms of her mommy for even more confirmation of her performance.

This little girl was so taken by the response to her performance that following her two sisters playing violin, she had to take another turn singing and playing the piano. The response from the audience to her second effort received even greater applause and approval.

There is a lesson to be learned here for the grown-ups. Everyone craves attention. Everyone wants their moment in the spotlight, their moment to shine. But when people do share their talents with us, they would like to be acknowledged and appreciated. Giving entertainers a thunderous round of applause does something very important. You are instilling within them the idea that they have value and that their life matters. I wonder how long celebrities would last if every time they gave a performance, their audience booed them off the stage?

This brings us to another lesson to be learned, that of dealing with disappointment.

How to Face Rejection

The best way to face rejection is to realize that it is impossible to please everyone all of the time. Everyone has different tastes. Everyone has different likes and dislikes. That means that if you take your talents to enough people, you will surely find someone out there in this big wide world that will like what you are doing.

I listened to one of Frank Sinatra's albums recently and something he said to a live audience struck me. He said, "I have never felt more love from an audience than I feel here tonight." I believe what he was really saying is, "I have never felt more people appreciating me performing my songs than I feel here tonight." Being acknowledged and appreciated is something that all people crave but seldom receive.

So if people should reject you instead of appreciating you, just realize that you are one step closer to finding those who will not only accept you but love whatever it is you are doing.

How to Stand Up and Speak in Front of People

For some, the prospect of standing in front of a group of people to speak to them is just about as scary as it gets. But doing such is no big deal, and it is no mean feat. Anyone can learn to do it.

Look Your Best

A good way to begin is to look your best. Get a new shirt and tie. Get a haircut. Be clean-shaven. Perhaps, purchase a new suit. For women, get a new blouse and scarf. Get your hair done in your favorite style. Perhaps, purchase a new dress. Doing these things, will give you the added confidence you will need to succeed. Always looking your best will keep your confidence in yourself strong.

Prepare Your Talk Before You Speak

Your talk can only be as good as the time you spend to prepare yourself for it. Begin by picking a subject on which to speak. A good idea is to make it a subject you have strong feelings and convictions about. You may wish to share a personal experience that teaches a principle about your chosen subject.

Make an outline of your thoughts and the points you wish to make. Now it is time to write and re-write, edit and re-edit. When you have done this at least four or five times and perhaps even nine or ten times your talk will have become the talk you will have hoped it would be. Once you have done all that initial work, God can inspire you and he will.

Keep Eye Contact with Your Audience

When you begin, look up over the heads of your audience should you have any thoughts of trepidation. Slowly bring your line of sight down to focus on the audience and then move your gaze from place to place in the audience.

Begin and continue speaking while making eye contact with your audience. Do not keep your head down buried in your notes. If you have to look at your notes, do so only briefly then make eye contact with your audience once again.

Your audience will be much more responsive to you if you keep your concentration on them and not on your notes. If you can memorize everything you wish to say, that is best of all. Your audience will be impressed and you will have no reason to break eye contact with them.

How old must you be to learn to speak before a crowd? The answer is, you can never be too young and you can never be too old.

Leaders Need God's Direction

If you are now seven years old or older, you may already hope to be a leader one day. The world needs the guidance and direction of

God more today than at any other time in the earth's history. How can any leader possibly believe that he or she is leading others or a nation by his or her own wisdom and understanding?

No one can do that. If you ever hope to be an effective leader, you must first acknowledge God and pray to God for his guidance, direction and wisdom. I quote from the book of Ecclesiastes once again: *"Let us hear the conclusion of the whole matter: Fear God and keep his commandments, for that is the whole duty of man. (Ecclesiastes 12:13).* And this: *"For God shall bring every work into judgment, with every secret thing, whether it be good, or whether it be evil" (Ecclesiastes 12:14).*

Children Can Learn How to Be Leaders

Children can encourage their parents to be better mothers and fathers by their example of being child-like, teachable, innocent, meek and lowly, clean, pure, and without sin.

Knowing that children are all these things, how is it that grown-ups do not ask the advice of children from time to time? Doing so could make the world a better place in which to live. Let us not forget that, out of the mouth of babes, wisdom and the words of eternal life have been spoken. (See Matthew 21:16).

Little children, teenagers and young

adults are the future of the world and that future is not coming, it is here now! These are the future leaders of the world.

Here are a few suggestions on how to be an effective leader:

To Be An Effective Leader, Tell People They Are Appreciated

Everyone enjoys being appreciated, including being told, "You are doing a good job." Have you ever thanked anyone for doing a good job? Be lavish with your praise often and show appreciation for a job well done often. But you must be genuine, and sincere, otherwise your words will mean nothing to those you praise.

One of my neighbors is a business owner. He is constantly giving luncheons and celebrations and showing many other manifestations of appreciation to his employees. Not only are the employees invited to these events but also added are customers, friends, relatives and friends of friends. Never once, have I heard this person correcting, scolding, or finding fault with an employee.

Instead, I did see him have an employee photographed with a story being written about him and placed on a brochure and inside of a magazine. In addition to this, his office door is always open. Who wouldn't want to have a boss and a leader like that?

Get down off your high horse folks, come back down to the planet earth with the rest of us humans. An effective leader does not strut around as if he is superior to all. If you think you are better than those you lead, you are not. You just have the privilege and opportunity to be in the limelight for now. But soon enough when you are no longer the leader and in the limelight you will, we hope, come back down to earth. Meanwhile, why not learn how to be an effective leader now?

An effective leader is an example of service and gratitude for those he leads. He is truly humble and then he has no guile. That is what makes an effective leader!

For the Leaders of the World

There will probably always be too many would be "chiefs" and not enough Indians. Unless you lead by example, perhaps, you should be made an example of. Unless you follow the example of the great exemplar, even Jesus Christ, you still have much to learn about leadership.

Be Humble

An effective leader is humble. Jesus got down on his hands and knees and washed the feet of his apostles to teach them humility. How many so-called leaders do we see doing anything remotely close to this? It is way past time that you continue to think of yourself as better or superior to those you may think you command, and begin thinking of yourself as a servant to all.

To all who are convinced that they are the elite and privileged and entitled people of the world, you are not! To all who believe you are VIPS, and the world revolves around you; you are not better than anyone else, you are simply in a position of privilege for now.

In the military, obedience and discipline are necessary, which requires deference from one person to another. But in every-day life, no one should assume superiority over another. The Savior of the world taught: "Blessed are the meek for they shall inherit the earth." (Matthew 5:5).

"But for the proud and the wicked (notice they are grouped together) they shall be as stubble. For behold, the day cometh, that shall burn as an oven; and all the proud and they that do wickedly, shall be as stubble: and the day that cometh shall burn them up, saith the Lord of hosts, that it shall leave them neither root nor branch" (Malachi 4:1).

I often see so-called bosses and leaders, standing around in groups of two and three observing the worker bees. Here's a novel idea and a news flash for you, you can preach a sermon without words, and that is to "pitch in and help."

If You Are Wrong Admit It

How refreshing it is to hear someone say, "I was wrong." Sometimes a newspaper or a magazine will have to print a retraction under threat of a lawsuit. That is not admitting you are wrong in the true sense of the word because the publication is being forced to admit they were wrong. But when anyone is able to say, "I was wrong and I take full responsibility for my mistake," that is refreshing to hear and it always will be.

Some may think that admitting you have made a mistake will detract from your credibility. On the contrary, doing such can only add to your credibility. People will begin to trust you and have confidence that you will always tell them the truth. Besides that, the ability to admit one is wrong is something that is seen so rarely in human beings today, it will assure you to stand out before the crowd.

Be Fifteen Minutes Early to All Important Meetings

I can always pick the potential leaders from any large group I am able to observe for more than one gathering. The potential leaders always arrive early and stay late. They ask intelligent questions and wait to get satisfactory answers. Then they repeat this pattern again and again.

Consider that you were leading an army of 10,000 men to battle and your army was all assembled and ready to face the enemy. But you arrive on the battlefield 20 minutes late! Many in the ranks may begin to say long before you arrive, "Where is our great and fearless leader?" There is no excuse for such behavior. And that is true.

If you are going to lead, you must be on time and not just on time but you must be early to everything. It is up to you to be out in front of those you lead setting the example at all times. It is you who should be waiting for your army to arrive and not your army waiting for you.

If you want to be an effective leader, be fifteen minutes early-to all, important meetings.

Go the Extra Mile

"And whosoever shall compel thee to go a mile,go with him twain" (Matthew 5:41).

There is more in that deceptively simple statement than meets the eye. It is one thing to do a task begrudgingly because you have been asked to do it. It is better to do the thing happily because you have been asked to do it. But it is best of all to do something on your own without having been asked.

Love Those You Lead

An effective leader is also loyal. He loves

those he leads, and asks God to protect them. There is a story about an Army colonel serving in Japan during World War II. He eventually found himself surrounded by the enemy who was on higher ground, which put him and his men in a very precarious situation. But the Army colonel began each day by going into his tent and reading the Bible and then getting down on his knees and asking God to protect the soldiers fighting in his battalion. As a result of his faith and prayers, not one man serving under his command was lost.

Great Leaders Inspire Others to Follow Them

Great leaders rise to the occasion, they take the initiative and make things happen! Outstanding leaders expect excellence but they do not achieve it by using fear and threats. They achieve excellence by setting the example and being excellent themselves. Great leaders go the extra mile, have courage, and they believe in their teams' ability to achieve excellence. They also allow their people to do what they do best.

Great leaders ask key people if they can get the job done and then they let them know they are counting on them and that they believe in them. Then, they let those key people go to work. Great leaders inspire others to follow them and ask of them, "what do you need?" We are here to help. Great leaders are followed in times of crisis because those around them believe they will win or die trying. Great leaders have great determination and great courage.

How to Get Things Done

It takes no skills or special talents to boss people. Anyone can do that, but no one likes to be told what to do. There is a fine line between telling someone what to do and asking them.

For example, "Check on this or that" is telling someone what to do. "Could you check on this or that for us?" is asking someone what to do. To be even more effective ask, "when you get a moment," or if time is a critical factor, "this needs attention right away, could you take care of it for us please?"

In the first instance, the person being asked could be made to feel like a slave without any ability to think, or act for himself. In the first example, the boss is not letting the worker feel like he has a choice in the matter. This is a mistake. In the second example, he who has been asked, is shown consideration and respect, and is made to feel like he has a choice.

Let Those You Supervise Feel They Are Working with You

That which also requires skill, is for a boss or a leader to make those he supervises feel as if they are working with him and not for him, for a common good, and a worthy goal. You may wish to begin by calling those in your employ or in your charge together and stating very clearly that they have been selected because you believe that they can and will get the job done. Let them know that you expect perfection but that they will be working with you and not for you to achieve it. Tell them clearly that your door will always be open.

An effective way to continue, with this goal in mind, is by recognizing workers when they arrive by saying hello and using their name. Should they be volunteers, it will be wise to thank them for coming. Be certain to also thank them for helping as they leave and speak their name, again. Everyone likes to hear their name when they are greeted or thanked. In other words, if you just blurt out commands, demands, and orders, those you supervise will think they work "for" you. That may work in the military, where obedience and discipline is necessary, but in civilian life, if you lead that way, the moment employees find another source of employment, where they are shown respect, consideration, and appreciation, they will be gone.

There is still more to do to allow people to feel as if they are working with you and not for you. Please do not forget to first acknowledge a job well done and then remember to reward a job well done.

Do Not Monitor

Do not monitor. Tell those in your charge

what needs to be done, then ask if they can do the job. When they acknowledge they can do the task, give the assignment. Then tell them you have confidence they will get the job done. Tell them you expect nothing short of perfection, then get out of the way and let them go to work. If you constantly look over someone's shoulder, you may as well do the task yourself because that behavior is telling the person you do not believe they can finish the task.

Give Those in Your Charge the Training They Need

You wouldn't send a commercial airlines pilot into the air with a plane-load of passengers without proper instruction. For example, the student pilot needs to make his solo flight. However, pilot trainees, must be instructed by a competent flight instructor.

The teacher should allow his student to ask questions and give him cautions so that he will not make mistakes. Ideally, the student will be taught to do his job so well that he will be able to teach others. When the instructor is confident his student is ready, the person in training must be given the opportunity to take his first solo flight.

Great leaders must do what seems to be a

complete contradiction. They must ask for perfection, yet allow those in their charge to make mistakes. We all learn by making mistakes.

For the Employees of the World

If you are approaching teen years, you will soon be seeking your first job. Consider what will be expected of all employees. Very often, we see workers in retail stores standing around talking to each other. Are you one who is giving an honest day's work, for an honest day's pay?

We have all seen employees talking to each other while you stand patiently waiting in front of them to be waited on. They will not even look up and acknowledge you are there until they finish their conversation. What is wrong with this picture? I have heard employees complaining and criticizing the company they work for in front of customers. This is not building up the image of the company and inspiring confidence in customers.

Every business owner and manager is constantly looking for employees who will be loyal and will not have to be told what to do more than once. Corporation CEO's, presidents, managers and business owners are all looking for self-starters who will go the extra mile and get the job done. They want employees who can motivate and inspire others to reach their quotas and develop new products and to make their company a national or even a world business leader.

The last thing corporations and companies, big and small, need, is someone who is tearing down the company and its management behind their backs. When leaders of men and industry finally find someone who not only understands these things, but also puts them into practice, that man or woman will be sought after by business owners, managers and CEO's from near and far. Employees must be trustworthy and honest. How many stories have you heard of employees stealing, or embezzling from their employers?

Just recently, I saw a big mess on the floor of a fast food establishment. This situation was dangerous, since a customer could slip and fall to the ground, even possibly resulting in a lawsuit. In addition, the mess was unsightly. Yet, no employee cleaned up the mess while we were there. My friend and I could not help but notice two employees finishing their workday, and walking right pass the mess as if it were not there.

All employees would be well advised to arrive at work early and stay a little beyond the quitting time. Don't be constantly looking at your watch and talking about how much time there is left until you get to go home, or when your vacation will begin, or when your next raise will come. When you arrive at the workplace, do not allow yourself to just stand around or sit and talk to other employees. Give a full day's work, for a full day's pay.

When you are asked to do something: do it. Do not ask "why?" Do not ask "how?" Do not ask for help or more pay, just get on the task and get it done. Don't worry about who will get the credit or how much it will inconvenience you, just get on the task and get it done.

The person who has asked you to do the thing may not know the words "please" and "thank you." You may never get a promotion or a raise in pay. Your boss or the person in charge may not appreciate what you have done or even notice what you have done but God will. And God will bless you by trusting you with more responsibility in doing His work and that is what counts the most!

Final Thoughts

Never underestimate the power of your own imagination. I believe if you can visualize your dreams, you can ultimately make your dreams come true. Now there is more to the formula or recipe for making your dreams come true than just this. You can review the first part of this book for those principles. But the power of your own "imagination" is the genesis. This is the beginning of everything.

You may think you will never make a difference. You may believe you are just one person with only one voice. Think again. God has given man dominion over the animals, the fowls of the air, and the fish of the sea. They do not have a voice but you do. If you choose to fear God and keep his commandments and love and serve all of God's children, you can have a strong voice for good. The things you say and do, can have great power to influence the lives of those who come unto the sound of your voice.

Let the greatest sermon you will ever preach be the silent sermon of your own life doing acts of kindness and lifting others out of the darkness and into the light. Doing such will allow the light that is in you to shine so brightly that the whole world will be able to see it.

Remember, Jesus has invited you to, "Let your light so shine before men that they may see your good works and glorify your Father which is in heaven" (Matthew 5:16).

The End

About the Author

Ronald H. Bartalini was born and raised in California. He has written two books of poetry, *"I Like You Because You Make Me Happy."* and, "Whispers and Sounds." He is also the author of, *"My Greatest Love, Missionary Stories from My Life," "Living With and Loving All of God's Children-A Primer For Youth-Musings on Manners and More,"* and "Hoppity Moose and the Red Caboose." He currently resides in Utah.

Captain's Log

Captain's Log

www.ingramcontent.com/pod-product-compliance
Lightning Source LLC
Chambersburg PA
CBHW060357050426
42449CB00009B/1778